True Stories BY GRANDPA

David Abshire
Illustrated by Louise Abshire

KITSAP PUBLISHING

True Stories By Grandpa
Second edition, published 2017

By David Abshire

Cover Design by Fusion Creative Works
Illustrations by Louise D. Abshire

Copyright © 2017, David Abshire

Hardcover: ISBN-13: 978-1-942661-63-4
Paperback: ISBN-13: 978-1-942661-12-2

All rights reserved. No part of this book may be reproduced or transmitted in any form or by any means, electronic or mechanical, including photocopying, recording or by any information storage and retrieval system, without written permission from the author, except for the inclusion of brief quotations in a review.

Published by Kitsap Publishing
1450 NW Finn Hill Road
P.O. Box 1269
Poulsbo, WA 98370
www.KitsapPublishing.com

Published and printed in the United States of America

TD 20170427

100-10 9 8 7 6 5 4 3 2 1

Grandpa wrote these stories for his four granddaughters, ages two to ten.

In June 1997 their father, an officer in the United States Air Force, was stationed in Naples, Italy for the duration of three years. It was Grandpa's goal to write and send his granddaughters one story a month while they were living there in order to stay in touch.

All of these stories are based on true events.

Table of Contents

Grandpa's Reading Glasses 1

The Really Dumb Big Fly 3

The Sunday Morning Chase 5

The Happy Little Family 8

Buddy Bandit 12

The Year Christmas
   Didn't Come 15

The Disappearing Wood 17

Grandma and the Really
   Mean Dog 20

The Littlest Brother 23

A Fishy Story 26

The Boy and the B-B Gun 29

The Crafty Little Donkeys 31

The Poor, Wounded Seagull 34

The Little Boy and His Bike 37

Yellow Lips Returns 39

Jimmy Crow 42

The Gift 45

Mighty Mouse 47

The Four Thieves 50

Visitors in the Night 53

Grandpa's Neighborhood 56

Grandpa and the Really
   Strange Deer 58

The Little Runt 61

The Gold Tooth 63

Rats 65

The Firecracker 67

Pat 69

The Little Bird 72

Old Scratchy 74

The Boy and the River 76

The Last Grizzly Bear 79

What If 81

Ice Cream 84

Grandpa's Reading Glasses

A True Story. By Grandpa.

One day Grandpa went to the bookstore and bought a book he wanted to read. He went home and sat down in his reading chair and reached for his reading 👓 on the lamp table. But, they weren't there. So Grandpa said to himself, "Hmm, maybe I left them in the office." So he went into his office. There were the office 👓, but no reading 👓. So Grandpa said to himself again, "Hmm, maybe I left them in the shop." So he went into his shop. There were the shop 👓, but no reading 👓. Grandpa checked his coat pockets. Not there. He checked in the bedroom. No reading 👓 again. He looked in the bathroom, on the TV, under his chair, in the front room, on the kitchen counter. Not there. He even checked out on the patio and once again, no reading 👓. Grandpa was really puzzled because his reading 👓 were always on the lamp table. Then he got a bright idea. "Maybe I left them in the pickup when I came home from the book store," he thought to himself. He got the pickup keys and went out and checked in the pickup. Not a bright idea. No reading 👓. He even checked Grandma's Jeep. Nope. By this time Grandpa forgot about reading his book. He wanted to find his reading 👓, just because he couldn't find them, but he didn't know where to look next. Grandpa said to himself, "Maybe Grandma knows where they are." He went into the kitchen where Grandma was working and said, "Grandma, I can't find my reading 👓 and I have looked high and low with no luck. Have you seen them?" Grandma looked up from kneading the bread she was making and just started laughing at Grandpa. Grandpa thought to himself, "What's so funny. Why is she laughing at me? This is serious. I can't find my reading ࿇." Then Grandma said to Grandpa, "Grandpa, put your hand on top of your head." So Grandpa put his hand on top of his head and guess what? There were the reading ࿇. They had been on top of his head all the time he was looking for them, and he felt really dumb. So now, when Grandpa can't find his reading ࿇, where is the first place you think he checks? ....

You guessed it…….. ON TOP OF HIS HEAD!

The End

The Really Dumb Big Fly

A True Story. By Grandpa.

One day when Grandma went to work she left Grandpa a "Daddy-Do list." One of the things on the list was to tie up a sagging limb on the dogwood tree. As he was tying up the limb, a really dumb big fly flew around the tree and accidentally hit Grandpa on the head, and he muttered under his breath, "What a dumb fly." The next day Grandma was cleaning around outside the house and put some stuff under the dogwood tree. As she walked back to the house a really dumb big fly flew around the tree and hit her on the head and she thought, "What a dumb fly." When she went back to put some more stuff under the tree she accidentally brushed against a limb and saw 6 or 7 really dumb big flies flying around the tree. She thought to herself, "Oh no, wasps! I'm going to get stung!" She ran faster than she thought she could to the back yard, and then sneaked into the house. She ran to the office, where Grandpa was working on the computer, and gasped that there was a wasp nest in the dogwood tree as big as a basketball. Grandpa said, "Oh, Gee," and went to investigate. He sneaked out the back door and very quietly and slowly approached the tree. He peered in through the branches and sure enough there it was, about eye level and hidden by leaves. He yelled back at Grandma that it was only the size of a volley ball and they weren't wasps but white faced hornets. She said the size of nest or the kind of bee didn't matter, they could still sting you.

So Grandpa went to the garden store and bought some hornet spray. That night when it got cool and dark he snuck out to the tree with his flashlight and hornet spray. Grandma was sneaking right behind him with her own flashlight to watch. He shined the flashlight into the tree and the nest was still there. He could see the hole where the hornets came and went, and standing in the hole were 3 or 4 big hornets looking back at Grandpa. He aimed the hornet spray at the nest and hole and let 'em have it. Dozens of hornets were just spewing out of the hole and falling dead to the ground. So Grandpa emptied the whole can on the nest and went back inside the house. The next morning he snuck out to the tree and with a big stick, poked the nest and luckily no hornets flew. He then cut the nest out of the tree and burned it in the burn barrel. The next time Grandpa and Grandma are walking around their yard and they get hit in the head by a really dumb big fly, they are going to run in the house as fast as they can go.

The End

The Sunday Morning Chase

A True Story. By Grandpa.

One Sunday morning Grandpa was reading the Sunday morning paper. He was half way through Garfield in the comic section when Grandma ran in the front door and said, "Grandpa, Grandpa, come and see." Grandma is always telling Grandpa to come and see something, so he got up and went to the front room. Grandma said, "Grandpa there's a cute little bunny rabbit out in the pumpkin patch and I think he's lost." So Grandpa and Grandma went out to the pumpkin patch and Grandma pointed to a big leaf on the pumpkin vine and said, "He's under there." So Grandpa slowly snuck over to the big leaf and looked under it. Sure enough there he was, a cute little yellow bunny rabbit looking back at Grandpa. Grandpa could see that the poor little bunny was blind in his left eye and should be easy to catch. So Grandpa slowly inched his hand down to catch the bunny, but the bunny hopped under another big leaf. Grandpa snuck over to the other big leaf to try and catch the bunny but the little bunny went hippity-hopping and hopped under Grandma's Jeep. When Grandpa reached under the Jeep to catch the bunny, the bunny went hippity-hopping back to the pumpkin patch. Grandpa told Grandma, "I can't catch the little guy."

And Grandma said, "What can we do?" Grandpa said, "Go knocking on the neighbors doors and see if anyone has lost a bunny." So Grandma went to the first house and knocked on the door and asked if they had lost a cute little bunny. They said no, so

Grandma went to the second house and knocked on the door and asked if they lost a bunny and they said no, too. Then Grandma went to the third, fourth and fifth houses and asked if they had lost a bunny, and they said no. At the sixth house Grandma knocked on the door and four little girls came to the door in their jammies and with no shoes on, and Grandma asked if they had lost a little bunny. All four girls said yes all at the same time and said they would come and catch him, and started out the door. Grandma said to them that they had better get some shoes on because the rocks at our house are pretty sharp. When the little girls had dressed themselves and put on some shoes they came over to Grandpa and Grandma's to catch the little bunny. At the same time all the other little kids that Grandma had knocked on their doors, came out of their houses, to see the bunny and help catch him. All in all there were twelve kids standing around in the pumpkin patch, and Grandpa was worried that they would trample all the pumpkins trying to catch the bunny, but they didn't. All the little kids started chasing the bunny trying to catch him. They chased him under the Jeep. They chased him into some bushes. They chased him under Grandpa's pickup truck. They chased him back

to the pumpkin patch, and then they chased him back into the bushes. They chased him all over the place, and after about forty-five minutes of chasing, Grandpa said, "Hold it." He told them that the little bunny was very scared and was trembling from all the chasing and that they would have to slow down in order to catch him. He also told them about the blind eye. Then one little boy snuck up on the bunny from the left side and slowly reached down and grabbed the tired and scared little bunny. All the little kids were happy and they took the bunny back to his cage and put him in with his mother and brothers and sisters. He was very happy to be home and not being chased by twelve kids. Grandpa and Grandma were happy too that all the little kids were out of the pumpkin patch.

The End

The Happy Little Family

A True Story. By Grandpa.

One day in early spring Grandpa was playing games on the computer and Grandma came in and said, "It's the first of March and the little swallows will be showing up from California soon so you better set up the little bird house." Grandpa said, "Good thinking, Grandma," and went out to the shed and got the little bird house. He took it down to the garden and put it up high on the pole. About a week later Grandpa was out on the patio and saw about ten little birds up in the sky darting around catching bugs to eat. Grandpa yelled into the house to Grandma, "I think the little swallows have returned." Grandma came out of the house and with Grandpa watched the little birds for a while. Sure enough the little swallows had arrived, and it was almost on the same day they arrived last year. Little swallows do that. Anyway, two of the swallows, a MaMa and PaPa, came down and sat on the roof of the birdhouse checking things out. Then they flew back up and joined the other birds catching bugs. Every day Grandpa and Grandma watched the little birds flying around catching bugs. Once in a while a sparrow or a wren family would try to move into the bird house and the PaPa swallow would chase them away. About a month after they had arrived MaMa swallow started taking pieces of dried grass into the house. She was building her nest. Every day she worked very hard flying in with the grass and flying out to find more. All this time PaPa swallow was sitting on the TV antenna on top of Grandpa's house, guarding the little bird house. That's the way they do it. MaMa builds the nest and PaPa guards it. About two weeks after she started on the nest MaMa swallow stopped taking in dried grass and instead started taking in white bird feathers. Grandpa figured she was just about done building and was making the nest soft for the little eggs and baby swallows that would soon be here. A few days later MaMa flew into the nest and stayed there for about an hour. Grandpa figured that she was laying eggs. A few days later Grandpa did not see MaMa swallow any more, but saw PaPa swallow sitting up on the TV antenna. Grandpa figured that MaMa was sitting on the eggs to hatch them. Then one day Grandpa saw MaMa swallow again but this time she was flying high up in the sky catching bugs and taking them down to the nest to feed the baby swallows. Every day MaMa would feed the babies all day long, and can you guess where PaPa was all this time? You guessed it, up on the TV antenna guarding the house. The baby swallows were growing every day and Grandma said she could hear the little birds going, peep, peep, peep. And soon the peeping turned into cheeping. Cheep, cheep, cheep. After the little birds got bigger they grew feathers and started sitting in the hole of the bird house waiting to be fed.

They took turns sitting in the hole. Grandpa and Grandma noticed that they all had different markings on their faces so Grandpa and Grandma gave names to all four of the little swallows. The biggest baby was named One Spot, the next one, Two

Spot, the third one, Black Eye, and littlest of the four was named Yellow Lips. MaMa kept feeding the little birds and soon they were big enough to fly. They would flap their wings all the time wanting to fly, but just couldn't make themselves jump out of the hole. Then one day One Spot jumped out of the hole and started flying. He flew straight up to where MaMa and PaPa were catching bugs and started learning how to catch bugs on his own. Soon Two Spot and Black Eye jumped out of the hole and flew up where One Spot had gone with MaMa and PaPa to catch bugs. They darted around playing tag and just enjoying flying with their new wings. But poor little Yellow Lips just kept sitting in the hole of the bird house, cheeping her little heart out. She wanted to join the others up in the sky but just couldn't make herself jump out of the hole and start flying. That evening the sun set and when Grandpa and Grandma went to bed, Yellow Lips was still sitting in the hole going cheep, cheep. The next morning Grandpa went out to check on Yellow Lips and figured that she had flown when the sun came up. There she was still sitting in the hole but not cheeping. She just sat there looking very sad. Grandpa said, "Come on Yellow Lips, you can do it," but Yellow Lips just sat there. Grandma went on her morning walk and Grandpa sat watching little Yellow Lips. Pretty soon MaMa swallow came down and made some cheeping noises at the little bird and flew back up to join the others. Yellow Lips just sat there and sat there looking up at her parents and brothers and sisters, watching them fly. Then, all of a sudden, Yellow Lips jumped out of the hole, made a right turn and flew right over Grandpa's head, then up over the house and straight up to where her family

was flying around. They all seemed so happy to see Yellow Lips flying and darted around chasing each other and having a good time. They never came back to the nest that summer but slept at night in trees somewhere. All summer long they flew around eating bugs and getting strong for the long flight home in the fall. Then one day Grandpa saw that all the swallow families had joined up. It was time to go. The next day Grandpa went out and all the swallows had left for California for the winter, and Grandpa yelled as loud as he could up in the sky, "See-ya next year, Yellow Lips!" Then Grandpa went down to the garden, took down the bird house, cleaned it and put it away 'til next spring.

The End

Buddy Bandit

A True Story. By Grandpa.

    One winter evening Grandma and Grandpa were watching Monday Night Football on TV. Suddenly Grandma turned to Grandpa and said, "Did you hear that?" Grandpa took off his earphones and said, "No, what did you hear?" And Grandma said, "I heard a noise." So they continued to watch the game. Suddenly Grandma turned to Grandpa and said, "I heard it again." Grandpa took his earphones off once more and said, "What did you hear?" And Grandma said, "A crunching noise out on the patio I think." Grandpa got up and went over to the back door and flicked on the outside light. The first thing he saw was a little raccoon scamper across the patio and into the bushes. He had been eating cat food from the cat food dish. When Grandpa told Grandma what he saw, she got up and got some more food for the cat food dish because it was very cold outside and animals need lots of food to stay warm. Grandma went outside and, when she knelt down to fill the dish, she saw what looked like a little pool of blood near the cat food dish. She said, "Grandpa, I think the little raccoon might be hurt. I wonder what happened to him?" Grandpa looked at the blood and said, "Maybe he got hit by a car or maybe a coyote got him." Grandpa and Grandma finished the football game and went to bed. The next night Grandma heard the crunching noise again. This time both Grandma and Grandpa went to the back door and flicked on the outside light. There was the little raccoon again, but this time he only scampered a few feet away and turned around and stared back at Grandpa and Grandma. They could see a round spot on his back where he had been wounded by something, but there was no blood. Grandma said, "He's so cute, he looks just like a little bandit." And Grandpa said, "Lets name him Bandit, Buddy Bandit."

All winter long Buddy Bandit kept coming back to eat cat food at the cat food dish and just loved Grandma's leftover waffles that she would feed him once in a while. Sometimes he would show up at night, and sometimes in the morning, and even a few times during the day. His wound healed up and new fur grew in. The new fur was a lighter color, so it was easy to tell it was Buddy Bandit. He got so tame that he would eat cat food right out of Grandpa's hand. Grandma told Grandpa that he shouldn't be feeding Buddy like that because after all he was still a wild animal and had very sharp teeth and claws. Buddy kept getting bigger and stronger all the time, and by springtime he was a very healthy raccoon. When the weather warmed up Buddy didn't come around as often, and after a while he didn't come to eat at all. Grandpa figured that he lived down by the creek and was eating regular raccoon food, like clams, shellfish, grubs, and so on. Then one morning Grandpa was playing with the computer and

Grandma came in and said, "Buddy Bandit is back eating cat food and he looks kinda skinny." So Grandpa went out on the patio and said to Buddy, "Where have you been and what have you been doing Buddy?" But Buddy just kept eating the cat food and Grandma gave him a leftover waffle which he took and ran off into the bushes. The next morning here came Buddy again for food and Grandpa and Grandma stood by the back door and watched him eat. Then they noticed a movement over by the edge of the patio. Out of the bushes came a little baby raccoon. Then out came another baby and another and another. Four little babies came walking across the patio to where Buddy was eating. They were little round balls of fur with little black masks and little black rings on their tails. Grandpa turned to Grandma and said, "Grandma, Buddy Bandit is not a boy raccoon at all, he's a girl raccoon, and she is a MaMa raccoon with four really cute little babies." And Grandma said, "She brought her babies back to show us." Grandpa and Grandma were so glad they could help Buddy make it through the winter and back to health. Buddy came back a few more times that summer with the babies, which were growing up fast. After a while Grandpa and Grandma didn't see Buddy or the babies anymore, and figured that the babies grew up and went their separate ways and Buddy went back to being a wild raccoon. Bye-bye Buddy Bandit. It was fun to know you.

The End

The Year Christmas Didn't Come

A TRUE STORY. BY GRANDPA.

One Christmas Eve, a long time ago, Grandpa had to work late and didn't get home 'til around midnight. When he pulled into the driveway he could see his three little kids looking out the front window. Grandpa went into the house and said, "How come you kids are still up? It's way past your bed time." The little kids replied, "We're waiting for Santa Claus." Then Grandpa said, "But Santa won't come unless you are in bed, asleep." So the three little kids went to their bedrooms and jumped into bed. But they didn't go to sleep right away. They just lay in their beds, talking back and forth, and giggling. Grandpa said, "You kids better get to sleep." Then Grandpa went into the front room and put a couple more logs into the fireplace and waited to make sure that the little kids settled down and went to sleep. The warm fire made Grandpa sleepy so he went into his bedroom and lay down on top of his bed, with his clothes still on, just to rest a few minutes. The next thing Grandpa heard was little kids whimpering and sobbing. He opened his eyes and saw that it was light outside. He thought to himself, "Oh no, I must have fallen asleep and its morning, Christmas morning." Then he looked over at the doorway and saw his three little kids standing there in their jammies, with tears in their eyes, and he asked them what was wrong. One little girl said, "Santa didn't come Daddy, there are no present's under the tree." So Grandpa jumped up. He didn't have to get dressed because he still had his clothes on. He said to the sad little kids, "Santa must have come. Maybe the fireplace was too hot so he left the presents someplace else." The little kids were still sad because they thought Christmas didn't come. So Grandpa said, "You kids wait here, and I'll go look around and see if I can figure this out." So Grandpa went out and looked in the garage. No presents. He looked all around outside the house. No presents. He even looked up on the roof by the chimney. No presents. Then he thought, "I haven't looked in the basement yet." So Grandpa went down the basement stairs, opened the door and turned on the lights. And what do you think Grandpa saw? Yes, presents. There were big presents, little presents, a bike, a trike and all kinds of toys. Grandpa thought to himself, "Santa left all the presents here in the basement so they wouldn't get wet and cold." Grandpa took all the presents upstairs and put them under the tree. The little kids were jumping up and down clapping their hands and smiling happy smiles because Christmas came after all. So, what do you think Grandpa should do different the next Christmas so that Santa can come down the chimney with the presents? That's right. He shouldn't put two more logs into the fireplace before he lays down to rest.

The End

The Disappearing Wood

A True Story. By Grandpa.

Between Grandpa and Grandma's house, and their neighbor's house, is a tall wooden fence. Along the wooden fence Grandpa stacks his winter firewood. The stack of wood is about as tall as a man and stretches all along the fence. As Grandpa uses the wood during the winter, the stack of wood goes down to nothing, and you can see the fence again. One year Grandpa was using the wood and the stack was going down, and Grandpa noticed a broken board in the fence. Since Grandpa babysits two little doggies once in a while, he left a small stack of wood in front of the broken board so the little doggies couldn't get out. One morning when Grandpa went out to get some wood for a morning fire he noticed that the stack of wood in front of the broken board seemed to be a little bit smaller. Grandpa thought, "HHMM," then grabbed some wood, went in the house and forgot about it. A couple days later Grandpa went out to the fence for wood and noticed that the little stack of wood was even smaller yet. He got some wood and went in the house and asked Grandma, "Grandma, have you been getting wood from the little stack of wood in front of the broken board in the fence?" Grandma said, "No, I haven't gotten any wood at all." So Grandpa thought, "HHMM." The next day Grandpa went out to get some more wood because it was really cold weather and he saw that even more wood was missing from the little stack. Grandpa thought to himself, "By golly, someone must be taking that wood. I'll have to watch it tonight." So that night Grandpa put on a nice warm coat, a warm hat, pulled on some gloves and went out by the fence and sat down and watched the little stack of wood. After about a half an hour Grandpa started getting really cold and was just about to go in the house when he thought he heard a noise on the other side of the fence. Grandpa sat really still and listened and listened. There, he heard it again. Someone was on the other side of the fence. Then Grandpa stared at the little stack of wood and noticed a movement through the broken board. Then a hand reached through the hole, followed by an arm. The hand reached down and grabbed a piece of wood and pulled it back through the hole. Then the hand came back through the hole again and grabbed another piece of wood. All in all the hand took four pieces of wood, and then it got real quiet outside. Grandpa went back into the house, took off his coat, stood by the stove to get warm, and told Grandma what he had seen. He said to Grandma, "Grandma, it appears that the neighbors are stealing firewood from us. That makes me mad. If they would just come over and ask for some

wood, we would give them more than enough because we have plenty. Tomorrow I'm going to move the little stack of wood and fix the fence so they can't take more." The next morning Grandpa did just that. He moved the wood back away from the fence and replaced the broken board with a new one so that no one could reach through the fence.

Did Grandpa do the right thing by fixing the fence so that no one could take his wood? Or should he have left it like it was, so the people could take wood to keep warm by, since he and Grandma had plenty? What do you think? What would you have done?

The End

Grandma and the Really Mean Dog
A True Story. By Grandpa.

Every single day Grandma goes for a morning walk, rain or shine. While on her walks she looks for money and nuts and bolts and anything else she can find just to make her walk interesting. She calls the things that she finds Road Kills. She also goes to the Post Office to get Grandpa's mail. So, on her daily list of things to do she writes P-O-R-K, or pork, which stands for Post Office and Road Kills. One day while Grandma was doing her PORK, a strange thing happened. As she approached the library she saw a big, old, mean looking dog sitting on the sidewalk. When Grandma got closer, the mean looking dog moved over onto the lawn and bared his teeth and growled at Grandma. Grandma always carries dog biscuits with her on her walks, and as she passed the dog she laid a dog biscuit on the sidewalk and kept going. After she got way past the dog she looked around and saw the mean looking dog eating the dog biscuit. The next day Grandma went on her walk and as she approached the library, there was the mean looking dog, again sitting on the sidewalk. As Grandma neared the dog he moved over onto the lawn but this time he didn't bare his teeth or growl at Grandma. When she passed the dog, she laid another dog biscuit on the sidewalk, and once again he went over and ate the biscuit after she had moved on.

Every day the mean looking dog waited for Grandma and her dog biscuits. Then one day after he ate the biscuit, he followed Grandma for a little while then sat down on the sidewalk. The next day he followed her again. After a few days the mean looking dog would come right up to Grandma to get his dog biscuit. He would walk right beside her as she continued on her walk. On her way home, when she passed the library, the dog would sit down on the sidewalk and watch her go home. Grandma told Grandpa about the dog and they figured that he was mistreated by someone and had run away from home. He was probably living in the woods by the library and just didn't like people, or was afraid of them. But since Grandma was nice to him and fed him every day he liked her. Grandma gave the dog a name. She called him Old Scruffy. Old Scruffy followed Grandma all the way home one day. Grandma said to Grandpa, "Old Scruffy followed me home. Come and look." When Grandpa opened the door Old Scruffy slunk back, lowered his head and bared his teeth at Grandpa and growled. After that he didn't follow Grandma home again. Everybody in town thought the dog belonged to Grandma because he walked with her all the time. One day when Grandma and Old Scruffy were walking past a store, a man in the store yelled out the door to Grandma and said, "Hey lady. You better do something about your dog. He's mean and he's going to bite somebody someday." And Grandma said, "He's not my dog. He just follows me around. He's my friend." One morning when Grandma got to the library, Old Scruffy was not there. The next day he wasn't there either. On the third day Grandma said to the man in the store, "My dog friend must have left." And the man said, "No, he was taken away. What happened was some boys were throwing rocks and sticks at him and he chased them barking and growling. Then someone called the people at the dog pound and they came out and trapped Old Scruffy and took him away." Grandma was sad to hear this and felt like she had lost an old friend. This little story just shows that if you are mean to animals you will make them mean. But if you are nice and loving to them, they will love you back. By the way, does anyone remember what P-O-R-K, pork, stands for?

The End

The Littlest Brother

A True Story. By Grandpa.

In every family that has more than one kid, there is always a little sister or little brother. But not everyone in the family has a little sister or brother. Look around your own family and see if you can figure out who doesn't. That's right. The youngest one. So this is a story about the littlest brother. One time there were three brothers. Big brother. Middle brother. And little brother. The three boys lived on a farm and had lots of work to do, which they called chores. They did their chores once in the morning and once at night. There were cows to be fed and milked. There were pigs to be fed and watered. There were chickens that needed to have their eggs gathered, and they also needed to be fed and watered. To make the work more fun the boys would make games out of their work. One game that they had the most fun with was riding the cows out of the barn after they had been milked. The way they did this was one brother would get on a cow's back and another brother would turn it loose. Now, cows are not horses and they don't like people on their backs, so when they were turned loose they would run real fast for the barn door and run out into the barn yard to get that thing off their back. The boys didn't ride them all the way out into the barn yard. They didn't because the barn yard was covered with cow poo and mud and water that would come up past your ankles if you walked in it, and they didn't want to get bucked off into that nasty place. So when the cows went through the barn door the boys just reached up and grabbed a board that went across the top of the door so they could slide off the cows back. Then they would go get on another cow and ride again until all the cows were out of the barn. Now, all the boys didn't ride the cows. Just the two bigger brothers. They wouldn't let the littlest brother ride because he was too small. But the littlest brother kept begging, "Let me ride one too." And the bigger brothers would say, "You're too little, little brother." Every night the little brother would beg to ride a cow. And every night the bigger brothers would say no because they didn't want him to get hurt. They knew that if he got hurt they would be in trouble. One rainy cold winter night when the boys had finished the milking, little brother just begged and begged and begged to ride a cow to the door. So the big brothers decided to let him try, since he wanted to so bad. They put little brother up on the back of one of the cows. Little brother was so happy to be able to ride a cow that he just grinned from ear to ear. Big brother turned the cow loose.

The big cow turned and headed for the barn door real fast with little brother bouncing up and down on its back. When the cow reached the door little brother put up his hands to catch the board. When the cow went through the door little brother was reaching as high as he could, but his hands just missed the board by about three inches, or about as long as your ear. He was too short! The cow sped out into the barn yard with little brother screaming at the top of his lungs. Then the big brothers heard, "KERRPLOP." They ran to the barn door to see if little brother was hurt, but they couldn't see anything because it was so dark. They got a flashlight and shined it out into the barnyard. There was little brother. He was sitting in the middle of the barn yard in all that goo and covered from head to toe with you know what. He wasn't smiling now. He was just sitting there crying. He wasn't crying because his body hurt. He didn't get hurt in the fall off of the cow's back. He was crying because his pride was hurt. Don't you think you would cry too, if you had all that yuckie stuff all over you? Well, little brother got a bath, had his hair washed and got clean clothes to put on. Yes, the big brothers got into trouble. But you know what? Little brother never asked to ride a cow again.

The End

A Fishy Story

A True Story. By Grandpa.

One time Grandpa went camping in the mountains. He didn't camp in a tent with a sleeping bag, but instead stayed in a nice, cozy little cabin with a fireplace, beside a mountain stream. It wasn't a big stream and it wasn't a little stream. It was just a nice medium-sized stream with lots of big rocks in it, with water swirling around them. Grandpa stood on the bank, looking at the stream and thought to himself, "I bet there's a nice trout behind every rock. This evening I'm going fishing." After dinner that evening Grandpa got out his fishing pole and fishing gear and went down by the stream. He selected just the right-sized hook and baited it with an egg and a worm. Then he cast the bait up stream and let it float down around the rocks. When it went around the second rock he felt a nibble and jerked up on the rod. Sure enough he had a fish on. The fish fought for a while and then Grandpa reeled him in. When Grandpa saw the fish he was disappointed. It was just a little trout not even big enough to keep. So he unhooked it and let it go. Grandpa kept fishing the stream and kept catching little trout and turning them loose. Then Grandpa thought to himself, "The sun is going down and I'm only catching little fish. I think I'll go down stream and find a nice big fishing hole." So he gathered up all his gear and walked down the trail beside the stream 'til he came to a nice big pool. The pool was pretty deep, with nice, clear, greenish water. It had logs and sticks along both banks. Grandpa thought to himself, "I bet there's some nice big trout under these logs." He baited up his hook again and cast it over to the other bank near the logs and let it sink.

Right away he felt a nibble and jerked up on the rod and reeled in. He had caught another little fish. He cast in again, and again caught a little fish. Grandpa thought to himself, "If I want to catch a big fish I better use a bigger hook and bigger bait." So he put a bigger hook on the line. Then he walked back up the trail to where he had seen some grasshoppers. He looked around until he found a nice big juicy grasshopper, about the size of your thumb, and caught it. He went back down to the pool and put the juicy grasshopper on the big hook. He then made a long cast over by one of the big logs in the water, and let it slowly sink down. The little trout tried to bite the bait but it was too big for their little mouths so they swam away. The bait kept sinking and sinking down to the bottom of the pool. All of a sudden Grandpa saw a big shadow move from under the sunken log. Wham! Grandpa's pole bent over double and started jerking like crazy. He had hooked into a very large fish. Grandpa tried to reel in the fish but the fish was so big that he swam downstream, and Grandpa couldn't stop him. Suddenly the fish turned and swam up stream with Grandpa fighting him every inch of the way. Grandpa got so excited that he stepped on a slippery rock and almost fell in the water. Back and forth the big fish swam, jerking the line and pole and jumping out of the water. When

Grandpa first saw him he thought that it was one of the biggest trout he had ever caught. It was about as long as from your finger tips to your elbow. After a while the fish got tired and Grandpa started reeling him in. Grandpa thought to himself, "Oh boy, trout for breakfast tomorrow morning." Then as Grandpa was raising the big fish over a log to the bank, the fish started flapping and jumping around like fish out of water do, and flipped himself right off the hook. Kerrplunk! Back into the water it fell and quickly swam under the big log on the other side of the pool, where he had come from. Grandpa sat down on a log nearby and just looked over to where the fish had gone. He thought to himself, "Big fish. I fooled you once but I'll never be able to fool you twice." Then Grandpa put a middle-size hook on his line and went up stream and caught some nice trout for breakfast. He felt bad that he had lost the big fish, but he was satisfied that he had out smarted the biggest trout he had ever seen. Isn't fishing fun?

The End

The Boy and the B-B Gun
A True Story. By Grandpa.

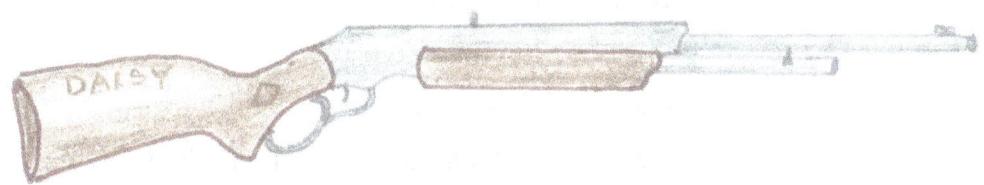

One time when Grandpa was a little boy he had a B-B gun. A Daisy, Red Rider B-B gun. All little boys, at that time, had Daisy, Red Rider B-B guns. Who knows why, but they did. Maybe it was because America was fighting World War II and everybody was super patriotic or something. Anyway the little boys would walk around shooting tin cans, glass bottles, and targets made of paper with bulls-eyes on them. B-B's won't kill people but they can hurt you, if you get hit by one. It feels almost like a bee sting. They can also put out an eye. One thing B-B's can kill, though, are little birds. The little boys quickly found this out and that's what they started doing, killing little birds. They started shooting sparrows because there were so many of them and they were in low bushes and hopping around on the ground. Then they started shooting other birds like swallows and wrens high up in trees and on telephone wires. One day one little boy had been out shooting birds with his friends. He was on his way home when he spotted a robin sitting on a fence. He put a B-B in his gun and aimed it at the robin. When the robin was in the sights he pulled the trigger. Bang! The boy looked up and saw the robin fall to the ground. The boy ran over to look at the robin. He knelt down by the robin and saw that it was dying. It was lying on its back with its little feet sticking straight up in the air and its eyes were closed. It had blood coming out of its little beak. The boy thought to himself, "What have I done? I just killed one of God's creations. A beautiful little bird. A robin. And for what? It can't be made into food. It wasn't bothering anybody. It was just going through life doing what robins do, building nests and catching worms and bugs." All of a sudden the boy felt really bad. He realized that he had just killed something for no reason, no reason at all, and he wished that he could bring the robin back to life just like it was before he shot it. But knew he couldn't. The boy picked up the dead robin and took it to the flower garden and buried it. He said a little prayer for the robin and placed a flower on the grave. That night the boy thought about what he had done. He decided not to go shooting birds for no reason.

   The boy grew up and he did go hunting, with a real gun for ducks, pheasants, grouse, and other game birds that could be used for food. But he never, ever, killed a robin again. So if you are ever outside and see a robin gathering worms in a lawn or sitting on a fence, think about that little boy and his Daisy, Red Rider B-B gun, and the lesson he learned that day.

The End

The Crafty Little Donkeys

A True Story. By Grandpa.
(As Told To Grandpa By Great Grandma)

 This story happened many, many years ago, even before Grandpa was born. Up in the San Gabriel Mountains above Pasadena, California, there was a gold mine. Because there were no roads in the mountains in those days you had to hike up a narrow trail which was located in a narrow canyon that had a small creek running through it. The man who owned the mine hired between twenty-five to thirty people to work in the gold mine for him. He had to feed them breakfast, lunch, and dinner because they all camped at the mine all week while they worked. The owner of the gold mine couldn't carry enough food to feed the workers because it took almost all day to hike to the mine from the store. He thought to himself, "I need some pack animals." So he went out and bought some little donkeys. Not just three or four donkeys, but fifteen or twenty donkeys. Donkeys make good pack animals for the mountains because they are strong, sure footed, and don't require a lot of food when on the trail. Plus, they are smart. Very, very, smart. Each little donkey had a backpack, which hung down on both sides of their backs. Then they were tied one behind the other so that they made up what looked like a train. A donkey train. That way the man could lead the little donkey train down the narrow trail to the store to get groceries. The man and the little train would leave the gold mine very early in the morning for town and wouldn't get back until it was almost dark. It was a long, long, hike, and the donkeys got tired, but they were tough and it didn't seem to bother them too much. One day the man was leading the donkey train back up to the gold mine from the store. About halfway home, one of the little donkeys slipped on a narrow ledge and fell into a large pool of water in the creek. The rocks were slippery and the little donkey had trouble getting his footing and floundered around in the water. Finally he stood up and got back on the trail. Now, it just so happens that this little donkey was carrying bags of sugar. And what happens when you put sugar into water? That's right, it melts. So when the little donkey was in the water all the sugar in his backpack melted and ran down stream. When the little donkey got back onto the trail he noticed that his backpack was very, very, light because all the sugar had melted. This, he didn't forget. On the very next trip the little donkey just happened to slip and fall into the pool again, but this time he had company. Some of the other little donkeys fell in too. Then on the next trip after that all the little donkeys were trying to fall into the water. The man didn't know what to do. He couldn't keep losing all that food, sugar, salt, coffee and stuff. He had to do something. Then he got an idea. He hitched up all the little donkeys and headed for town. When he got there he loaded up all the little back packs with large dry sponges. When the donkey train got to the pool on the way back to the mine all the little donkeys fell into the pool once again and their back

packs and sponges got very wet. Now, what happens when you put a dry sponge into water? That's right. It soaks up the water and becomes very heavy and that's just what happened to the sponges the donkeys were carrying. Now the donkeys had to carry really heavy loads and the water was dripping from the sponges onto the trail making it muddy and slippery. The man made the little donkeys carry their heavy loads all the way back to the gold mine like that, and it was not a fun trip. The donkeys didn't forget, and after that they never fell into the water again.

The End

The Poor, Wounded Seagull

A True Story. By Grandpa.

One time Grandpa and Grandma took a long, long car trip from their home in Washington clear across the United States to the State of New York. They saw all kinds of neat things along the way, like some deer, an elk, a large herd of buffalo, a little herd of antelope, and even a bear. When they got to New York they rented a room in small motel on the shores of Lake Champlain. One morning Grandpa went out to his car to get something and noticed a lady feeding a seagull out in front of her motel room. Grandpa could see that the seagull was dragging one wing on the ground when he walked around, so Grandpa figured he had a broken wing and couldn't fly. The next day Grandpa and Grandma went outside and there in the middle of the parking lot was the poor little seagull hopping around, dragging his wing, looking for food. Grandpa said to Grandma, "There's that poor little seagull I told you about. Do we have any extra food for him to eat?" Grandma said, "Yes, we have a loaf of bread. I'll go get a slice." So Grandma went into the motel room and got a slice of bread. She came back out and gave the slice of bread to Grandpa so that he could feed the poor little seagull. Grandpa pulled off a piece of the bread and tossed it on the ground. Right away the little seagull hopped over and gobbled down the piece bread. Grandma said, "He really looks hungry." So Grandpa pulled another piece of bread off the slice and tossed it on the ground. But this time he didn't toss it as far and the little seagull hopped over and gobbled that one up. Each time Grandpa tossed a piece of bread he would make it land closer to him and Grandma. Each time, the little seagull hopped closer and closer, gobbling up the bread until he was only about four feet away from them, but he would come no closer. The little seagull ate the whole slice of bread. The next morning Grandpa and Grandma went out to feed the little seagull and this time they took a handful of oatmeal cookies because they thought that would be better food than just a plain slice of bread. There in the middle of the parking lot was the little seagull hopping around looking for food. When he saw Grandpa and Grandma he came hopping over, dragging his wing, to within about four feet of them. Grandpa and Grandma broke the cookies into small pieces and put them on the ground and stepped back. The little seagull hopped over and ate every single piece of the cookies. Grandpa said, "I hope someone feeds this poor little thing after we leave, so that he can stay alive." On the morning that Grandpa and Grandma were going to leave for home, Grandpa went out to feed the poor little seagull one last time. But this time the poor little seagull was not in the parking lot. Grandpa looked all over but no little seagull. Grandpa was worried that something might have happened to him. Just then a beautiful seagull came gliding down out of the sky and landed in the middle of the parking lot. As soon as he landed he stuck one wing down on the ground and dragged it when he came hopping over to Grandpa. Grandpa said to himself. "That's the poor little seagull. He's not wounded at all. He can fly." Grandpa gave the cookies to the seagull anyway and went back into the motel room. He said to Grandma, "Grandma, we've been fooled. That poor little seagull can fly. He just dragged his wing on the ground so that we would feel sorry for him and give him food, and it worked." What did Grandpa and Grandma learn from this seagull adventure? DON'T BELIEVE EVERY THING YOU SEE.

The End

The Little Boy and His Bike

A True Story. By Grandpa.

In a small town in California there lived a little boy and his family. He had an older sister, a younger sister, a MaMa, and a PaPa. Out behind the little boy's house was an alley. At the end of the alley was a street that was busy with cars. Not very many cars drove through the alley, so the little kids would play there with their bikes and trikes and wagons. The little boy didn't know how to ride a bike yet so he asked his PaPa to teach him. The bike didn't have training wheels, so PaPa had to run beside the bike, holding it, to keep the little boy from falling over. Up and down the alley they would go, the little boy trying to learn how to ride, and PaPa running beside him. PaPa would get really tired, but one day the little boy finally learned how to ride the bike. He would ride back and forth in the alley every chance he got, because it was so much fun. He rode slowly at first, but as he practiced he rode faster and faster until he was really speeding along. One day PaPa saw the little boy ride out into the street at the end of the alley without checking for cars first. So PaPa sat the little boy down and told him that he had to ride the bike in a safe manner or he might get hurt. He told the little boy that when he came to the end of the alley, he had to Stop, Look, and Listen for cars before riding out into the street. PaPa asked the little boy if he understood, and the little boy nodded his head that he did. One day after school the little boy was riding the bike in the alley and he forgot to Stop, and he forgot to Look, and he forgot to Listen. He didn't see the car coming down the street. BANG! The little boy ran right smack into the side of the car and fell off of his bike into the street. The car stopped and two people got out to see what had happened. The little boy's sisters, seeing all this happen, ran into the house and told their PaPa that their brother got hit by a car. Well, PaPa was really scared what might have happened to the little boy, and he ran out the back door and into the alley. The first thing that he saw was the two people bending over the little boy. The little boy was just sitting in the street beside his bent up bike holding his nose. PaPa checked the little boy over and found that he only had a bloody nose and no broken bones, scrapes, or bruises. He was very lucky to not have gotten hurt more seriously. After that, when he was riding his bike, the little boy never forgot those three very important words his PaPa told him. Do you remember what those words are? ...... That's right. STOP, LOOK, and LISTEN.

The End

Yellow Lips Returns

A True Story. By Grandpa.

One spring day, the next spring after the Happy Little Family of swallows had left for California for the winter, Grandpa once again got out the birdhouse and put it up on the tall pole in the garden. It was the first day of March and he knew that the little swallows would be returning from California soon to build nests and raise baby birds, like they do every year. About the middle of March Grandpa and Grandma were out weeding the gardens, and Grandma looked up in the sky and said to Grandpa, "Grandpa, I think I just saw a swallow." Grandpa looked up and sure enough, there, way up in the sky were two little swallows flying around catching bugs. Pretty soon more and more swallows kept arriving until there were more than a dozen flying around. After a while two of the swallows flew down and landed on the birdhouse to claim it for themselves as their home for the summer. Other swallows flew down and tried to take the house away from the first two but they were chased away every time they got too close. Then Grandpa noticed that one of the two little birds had a yellow beak. Grandpa said to Grandma, "I think that's Old Yellow Lips Grandma. What do you think?" Grandma looked and said, "I think you are right Grandpa. That has to be Yellow Lips, and she brought a mate with her to raise a family." All that spring the two birds did what swallows do, darting around in the sky, catching bugs, and guarding their house. After a while, Yellow Lips started filling the house with twigs, pieces of grass, and string. She was building her nest. All the time she was working on the nest, her mate would sit up on the TV antenna guarding the house like papa swallows do. Grandpa knew she was about done building when she started taking white feathers in to soften the nest. Soon she laid her eggs and started sitting on them to hatch them. In about two weeks Yellow Lips was out flying, but this time she returned to the nest again and again with bugs in her beak to feed the baby birds. The baby birds grew and grew and were soon sitting in the hole of the birdhouse and Grandpa knew it wouldn't be long before they would be flying. One morning as Grandma was leaving on her morning walk she saw two of the baby swallows leave the nest and fly up to where Yellow Lips and her mate were catching bugs. The other two little birds stayed in the nest because they just weren't quite ready to fly yet. That afternoon some big black clouds moved into the area bringing with them lightning, thunder, and heavy rain. Then the storm began. The lightning cracked, the thunder boomed, and the rain roared down. All the swallows up in the sky flew away and found safe shelter from the storm somewhere, and Grandpa figured the two little birds in the birdhouse would be okay, if they just stayed there.

All afternoon the rain fell and the wind blew and everything got soaked. Then, as fast as it had come, the thunderstorm left and the sun started to shine. All the swallows returned to catch bugs that the storm blew in. Grandpa put on his coat and went out to check on the little birds in the birdhouse. When he got down to the garden he saw a very sad sight. There on the ground below the birdhouse lay the two little swallows. They didn't make it through the storm. Grandpa told Grandma that he thought that they must have tried to fly during the worst of the weather and the wind and rain knocked them to the ground. Grandma said, "Poor Yellow Lips lost two of her babies." And Grandpa said, "I know, but she still has two that made it." At the end of that summer, before winter arrived, Yellow Lips, her mate, and the two remaining babies joined up with all the other swallows in the area and flew south to warmer weather. Just like the year before, Grandpa took down the birdhouse, cleaned it and put it in the shed, knowing that the little swallows will be back again next year.

Grandpa wrote kind of a sad story here but it's a story from which we can all learn a lesson. Can you guess what that lesson might be? Yup. WE SHOULD ALL STAY IN THE HOUSE DURING A LIGHTNING AND THUNDER STORM.

The End

Jimmy Crow

A True Story. By Grandpa.
(As Told To Grandpa By Great Grandma)

Do you remember the story about the Crafty Little Donkeys? About the same time of year that the crafty little donkeys were falling in the water in that story, a gold miner in the same area decided to build his growing family a new and bigger house. The miner's family consisted of his wife, three boys, one little girl, and a baby on the way. They wanted the house to be out in the country so they could start a farm and raise animals. The miner hired some carpenters to build the house. They built the foundation and floors, and put up the walls and roof. They put in the stoves and sinks and painted the walls. There were no windows put in yet and no doors on the closets or pantry. Even though the house was not done yet, the miner moved his family in anyway, because they needed more space. In the same neighborhood that they built their house, lived someone else. That someone else was a crow. Jimmy Crow. Jimmy Crow would fly in through the unfinished windows and help himself to food off of the table and counters and even off the stove sometimes. He loved bright and shiny things and all kinds of small objects, and it was suspected that he might be taking some of these things with him. One day, even though the house wasn't finished, the MaMa decided to have a tea party for some of her friends. She put on her apron to make some sweet rolls, tea cakes and cookies. She took off her engagement ring, the one that had the diamond in it, because she didn't want to get dough stuck in it. She did the baking, made the tea, then took off her apron to greet her friends when they came. After the tea party she went to the kitchen and cleaned up. After the last dish was put away she looked for her ring but it was not where she thought it was. She looked everywhere but could not find it. Then she thought, "Jimmy Crow! Jimmy Crow has taken my beautiful ring. Now I'll never get it back." She told the boys what had happened. She asked them if they thought they could find Jimmy Crow's nest and see if he took the ring back there. The boys looked all around for Jimmy Crow's nest. They finally found it high up in the barn above the hay loft. The boys climbed a ladder up to where the nest was located. When they looked in the nest their eyes almost popped out. There in the nest were thimbles, small spoons, bright scraps of cloth, sewing needles, knitting needles, marbles, pins, and all kinds of small stuff. They looked and looked but no diamond ring. When they told their MaMa that they didn't find the ring in the nest she was just heartsick. Now she knew that she would never see the ring again. She felt hatred in her heart for Jimmy Crow and vowed she would wring his neck, if she ever got her hands on him. A couple of weeks went by and MaMa decided to have another tea party for her friends. She put on her apron to get ready to make sweet rolls, tea cakes, cookies and tea. When she reached her hand into the pocket of the apron she felt something. Then her eyes got wide and her mouth flew open, because she knew that what she felt was her missing ring. She was a very happy lady, now that she had her lovely ring back. She had forgotten that she had put the ring in the pocket of the apron instead of up on the windowsill like she thought she had done. Now she didn't hate Jimmy Crow anymore, even though he was still a pesky little thief.

The End

The Gift

A True Story. By Grandpa.

Christmas was rapidly approaching and the mother of a little girl didn't know what she was going to do for a gift for her little daughter. The father was out of work so they didn't have a whole lot of money to buy presents for each other. A neighbor lady had given the mother a big box full of scraps of yarn but there wasn't enough yarn of any one color to knit anything of any size. The little girl badly needed a sweater to wear to school because it was quite chilly outside. The mother looked at all the scraps of yarn and thought to herself that a sweater of different colors wouldn't look too good. Then she got a good idea. She decided that a poncho of lots of different colors might work. The mother started knitting the little poncho using all the different colored yarn that was in the box. She worked on it during the day when the little girl was in school and at night when the little girl was asleep. Finally the poncho was finished and the mother wrapped it in pretty paper and put it under the Christmas tree. Christmas morning came and the little girl opened her present from her mother. When she saw the poncho she thought it was the most beautiful thing she had ever seen. She tried the poncho on and it fit just right. All the colors looked so good and it even had a long fringe at the bottom of it. It was nice and warm too. After Christmas vacation the little girl wore her new poncho back to school. All the other little girls in her kindergarten class thought the poncho of many colors was very pretty and all of them wanted to try it on. The little girl wore the poncho all through kindergarten and all through the first grade. Finally, as the little girl grew older, the poncho became too small for her to wear so she handed it down to one of her smaller cousins. The cousin wore the poncho for a couple of years and she also grew too big to wear it any more so she handed it down to another cousin, and that cousin passed it down to someone else. The poncho that the little girl loved so much finally went to the Goodwill store and nobody knew what happened to it after that. A few years later the little girl's mother got a job working at the school. One day she was out on the playground watching all the little kids at play during recess. Over in the corner of the playground she saw that a bunch of girls had crowed around one little girl who was poor and not very popular, and went over to see what was going on. When she got there she couldn't believe her eyes. The little poor girl was wearing the poncho of many colors, and all the other little girls thought it was beautiful and wanted to try it on too. The mother was happy to see that the poncho was still in good shape and was still being used by someone who really needed it. Grandpa always wondered what might have happened to the little poncho of many colors, when the little poor girl couldn't wear it anymore. Maybe it was handed down to some other little girl who needed it. Or, maybe it went back to the Goodwill store. Who knows? What do you think might have happened to that pretty little poncho of many colors?

The End

Mighty Mouse

A True Story. By Grandpa.

I bet you think this is a story about a big mouse or a super mouse or something. But it's not. This is a story about a little racehorse. A very special, little racehorse. Years ago, Grandpa got a chance to buy a racehorse. The horse didn't cost a lot of money because he was small for a racehorse and he didn't look like he could win even a single race. He wasn't tall and long and pretty like most racehorses. He was kind of short and stocky, and his color was gray, just like a mouse. His racing name was Romper Deck, but his nickname was Mighty Mouse, which everybody called him. Anyway Grandpa bought the horse, hired a horse trainer to teach the little racehorse how to race, and hired a jockey to ride him. All summer long the trainer and jockey worked with Mighty Mouse to get him ready for racing at the big racetrack. They fed him special oats and hay and gave him special shots to keep him healthy. Every day Mighty Mouse worked out. He had to learn how to jump out of the starting gate at the beginning of the race. He had to learn how to run very fast against other horses. And he had to learn to keep running as fast as he could until he reached the finish line. After all the training he did, his muscles got stronger. He could run a long ways without getting winded, and he was healthy as a horse. Just before it was time to go to the big racetrack in the big city, the trainer took Mighty Mouse to a small racetrack to run against other horses that were also in training. Grandpa got nervous when he saw the horses that Mighty Mouse would be racing. They were big, strong looking animals, and Grandpa just knew that poor little Mighty Mouse was going to get left in the dust. Soon it was time for the race. The jockeys got up on their horses. All the horses were loaded into the starting gates. Everybody was nervously waiting for the starting bell. CLANG. The starting bell rang, the gates opened and they were off in a cloud of dust. Grandpa couldn't see Mighty Mouse and had a sick feeling in his stomach that the little horse was left far behind by the bigger horses. Then Grandpa saw him. He was right in the middle of all the horses. His eyes were wide and his nostrils were flared open and he had kind of had a wild look on his face. As soon as all the horses fanned out Mighty Mouse saw an opening and took off. He passed one horse and then another horse, until he was tied for first with a big black horse with a white streak on his face. They ran side by side for a while. Then Mighty Mouse just took off and left all the other horses behind. Nobody could believe that the little horse won the race. No, Might Mouse wasn't big, and he wasn't beautiful, but he had something that a lot of the other horses didn't have. He had spirit. The will to win that was in his heart, a will that could not be taught by a trainer or a jockey. Well, Mighty Mouse went to four more little racetracks in four more little towns and won every single race he was in. Grandpa was very proud of Mighty Mouse and was very excited about taking him to the big racetrack. Then one night Mighty Mouse was in his stall resting after a race. Unknown by anyone, one of his horseshoes had come loose and turned outward. As he walked around in his stall the shoe kept cutting his other leg. The next morning the trainer saw the cut and called the vet. The vet came and treated the cut and put a bandage on it. But the wound developed an infection and the vet had to cut some of it out. The vet told the trainer that because of what he had to cut, the little horse would never be able to race again. He could be a saddle horse but he could not run in races. So Grandpa had to sell Mighty Mouse because Grandpa didn't have a place to keep him. Grandpa was sad that Mighty Mouse would never race again but he was happy to have owned the greatest little racehorse he had ever known. So now, whenever we think that there is something that we can't do, or something we're afraid to try, we should think of that little horse with spirit. Spirit, and the will to win.

The End

The Four Thieves

A True Story. By Grandpa.

A long time ago there were four young boys who lived in the same neighborhood and were in the same grade at school. It probably was the fourth grade. Anyway, the boys played together all the time. They rode their bikes together, they played cowboys and Indians together, and went swimming in the river together. One summer, when school was out for summer vacation, the boys were having a grand old time doing what boys do, and just enjoying not having to sit in a hot classroom all day. Down near the swimming hole in the river where the boys went swimming was a little farm. Old man Campbell's farm. Now, old man Campbell was a mean looking guy and the boys were afraid of him. They never went near the farm when they went swimming and always avoided old man Campbell. Old man Campbell didn't have a wife or children and he was kind of dirty looking because he was working in the dirt, growing things all the time. One thing that he grew was cantaloupes. He had a huge patch of cantaloupes. The cantaloupe patch was located down by the river and they were the biggest, juiciest looking cantaloupes you have ever seen. Now, I said that the boys never went near old man Campbell's farm. But one time they did. The boys figured that they could crawl into the brush by the river and then crawl on their stomachs into the cantaloupe patch and eat some cantaloupes, and old man Campbell would never see them. And they did just that. They crawled into the cantaloupe patch and filled their bellies with ripe juicy cantaloupes and then

crawled out of the patch. And they were right, old man Campbell never saw them. The plan worked so well that the next day they did the same thing again. They figured that they had found the best thing since ice cream was invented. On the third day the boys crawled into the patch and were enjoying a feast of cantaloupes when one of the boys heard a noise. He looked around and let out a loud scream because standing over him was OLD MAN CAMPBELL and he had a big weed hoe in his hands. The boys were scared out of their wits and knew for sure that old man Campbell was going to kill them right there in the cantaloupe patch. But old man Campbell wasn't frowning and didn't seem mad. Old man Campbell had a smile on his face and was chuckling to himself. Then he said, "Boys, I've been pretty busy this summer growing fruits and vegetables to sell to stores and I've gotten behind on my weeding. So I figured you've eaten about ten dollars' worth of cantaloupes there, and at one dollar an hour you each owe me two and one half hours of work to pay for the fruit you have eaten." So old man Campbell led the boys up to the tool shed and gave them each a weed hoe and put them to work weeding the cantaloupe patch. As old man Campbell watched, the boys worked. It was hot and dusty and the work was not fun at all. After two and one half hours old man Campbell said, "Okay boys, I think we can call it even. You can quit now." As the boys were leaving, old man Campbell said to them, "You boys come back and weed anytime and you can eat all the cantaloupe you want. And just remember, nothing in life is free. You have to pay for everything you take." Now, Grandpa thinks the four thieves learned a good lesson that day. And Grandpa says that if you are going to steal, you better have a good time doing it, because sooner or later you're gonna get caught. And that WON'T BE FUN.

The End

Visitors in the Night

A True Story. By Grandpa.
(As Told To Grandpa By Great Grandma)

Way back in the old, old, olden days, Grandpa's Great-Great Grandfather moved from New York State to the wilds of Canada, above New York. His plan was to clear the land, build a log cabin, and start a farm to make a living and to raise his family on. He left his little family in New York until he had a place for them to live. The land was wild but fertile, and the neighbors were few and far between. Great-Great Grandfather started cutting down trees to build the cabin. The little log cabin was going to be small at first but he knew he could add on rooms, once he planted the crops and moved his family in. All during the springtime he cut big logs for the walls and smaller logs for the rafters and beams, and slowly the little cabin began to take shape. He built a stone fireplace for cooking and cut cedar shingles for the roof. After the roof was on and no leaks could be found he started making beds and tables and chairs out of wood. The last thing he made for the cabin was a heavy, but very nice, front door to keep critters out so they wouldn't steal food. Now the little log cabin was done. Well, not quite done. There was no glass for the windows. Glass was very expensive, so he decided to get the glass later before winter set in. Every morning at sunrise Great Great Grandfather would go out and work the land and plant the crops. He worked hard all day and at sundown he would go back to the little cabin and cook his dinner in the stone fireplace. Because there were only candles to burn for light at night, and because he had worked hard all day, he usually went to bed very, very, early. One night he went to bed and was just about asleep when he heard a noise way off in the distance. It sounded kind of like a dog or coyote howling. There, he heard it again, but only this time it was a little closer. Oow-oow-oooww. Oow-oow-oooww. Great-Great Grandfather sat up in bed because what he was hearing was not a dog, and was not a coyote. It was a pack of hungry WOLVES and they were headed in his direction. He thought, "Oh no, there's no glass in the windows and I only have a few bullets for my gun. I've got to hide because they might come in here looking for food." With that he jumped up out of bed and pulled on his clothes, all the while listening to the wolves getting closer and closer. Oow-oow-oooww. Oow-oow-oooww. He climbed up into the rafters of the little cabin

and hid way over in a corner so the wolves couldn't see him if they came in. It was very quiet now, and nothing could be heard but the beating of his heart. All of a sudden he heard a scratching noise just outside one of the open windows. Then in the moonlight he saw a dark figure leap through the window onto the cabin floor. Then another and another until five big hungry wolves were standing in the middle of the little log cabin. Great-Great Grandfather was very scared now, and sat very, very still and didn't make a sound. The wolves started sniffing around the cabin for food. They ate what was left of dinner at the fireplace and table. Then they tore open the food box eating anything and everything they could find. They even tore open the bed looking for the man that had just been in there. After they were satisfied that there was no more food to eat the wolves jumped back out of the open window and were gone. Great-Great Grandfather stayed up in the safety of the rafters all night until daybreak and then climbed down to clean up the mess the wolves had left. Because the wolves had eaten all of his food, Great-Great Grandfather set out for New York that day to get more food supplies and to pick up his little family. You can be sure he also bought some window glass to bring back to the cabin too.

The End

Grandpa's Neighborhood

A True Story. By Grandpa.

We all live in neighborhoods, of some sort, with all kinds of different types of neighbors. In Grandpa's neighborhood there are lots of good neighbors. Grandpa never visits with his neighbors because this is a different kind of neighborhood. This is Grandpa's backyard neighborhood of birds and animals and all kinds of critters. Grandpa's favorite neighbors are the little Swallows that return every year, at the same time, to build nests in the birdhouses to raise their babies. They fly around in the sky catching bugs and insects to eat, which is good because some of the insects are mosquitoes, and Grandpa doesn't like mosquitoes. Another fun neighbor is the Raccoon who comes to the cat food dish by the back door to steal food. The Raccoon is a very messy eater. She can't eat out of a dish like a dog or cat because her nose is too long and her mouth can't reach the food. She picks up the food with her front paws and stuffs it in her mouth. Then she starts chewing and crunching away with her mouth open and some of the food falls back out of her mouth onto the ground. Not a very polite way to eat at all, but still she's a nice neighbor. Across the street and high up in a big fir tree lives a family of Crows. Now, Grandpa doesn't necessarily like this family of Crows, because they sometimes mess up his garden. When Grandpa plants his corn and beans, and when the new little plants begin to grow, the crows fly down and pull up the little plants to eat the tender seeds that are still attached to the baby plants. Then Grandpa has to go back out and replant the garden. These are not very nice neighbors at all. But probably the nicest neighbors in the neighborhood are the Robins.

    Mama Robin built a nest somewhere in the back yard but she hid it so well that Grandpa couldn't find it. The Robins are very quiet birds. They hop around the garden eating bugs and worms. They also have a taste for Grandpa's blueberries and Grandma's cherries. But that's okay. There's enough to share. And then there's one neighbor that doesn't like Grandpa very much at all: the Blue Jay. The Blue Jay comes down out of the mountains every fall to spend the winter. He thinks the whole neighborhood belongs to him, so when Grandpa walks around in the backyard, the Jay sits up in the trees and chews Grandpa out for being there. Grandpa yells back, "I was here first," but the Jay just keeps squawking away. Grandpa's backyard neighborhood consists of many, many more birds and insects, like Hummingbirds, Nuthatches, Varied Thrushes, Ladybugs, Butterflies, Bees, Dragon Flies, Hornets, Wasps, Flies, and so on. All are fun to watch.

So, now Grandpa is curious. What do you have in your backyard neighborhood? Do you have fewer neighbors or more neighbors than Grandpa? Someday you should go out in your backyard and take a good look around and write down what you see or have seen. Happy bird and critter watching, kids.

The End

Grandpa and the Really Strange Deer
A True Story. By Grandpa.

One summer Grandpa and Grandma rented a house at Sunriver, Oregon. It was a very nice house set in among pine trees with wild bushes all around and patches of tall native grasses. There weren't very many houses nearby so it was nice and quiet and peaceful. Once in a while, though, a train would go by on the railroad tracks up on the hill but it wasn't very noisy and didn't bother them much. Even when she is on vacation Grandma always goes on her morning walk. One particular morning after Grandma had left, Grandpa went out on the back deck and sat in the sun to read his paper and sip his morning coffee. Grandpa sat there for a while reading and sipping his coffee when he heard a noise over by the trees. Grandpa looked around but didn't see anything so he kept reading. Thud. There was that noise again. "What could it be," Grandpa thought. Grandpa got up and took a closer look over by the trees. Thud. Grandpa discovered what the noise was. A big gray squirrel was sitting up in a pine tree eating pine cones and dropping them on the ground. Grandpa sat down again to finish his paper. After a while Grandpa thought he saw something out of the corner of his eye. He slowly looked around and there, just a few feet away, was a large female deer, looking around the corner of the house and staring at Grandpa. Grandpa sat there real quiet and stared back. The deer stood there with her big ears sticking straight up and her big eyes wide open. She just stood there and didn't move and kept staring at Grandpa. Grandpa just sat there staring

back and wondering what the deer was going to do. After a few minutes of staring, the deer moved on into the bushes and tall grass eating as she went along.

   Grandpa watched her until she wandered out of sight then he finished his paper and went into the house. Just then Grandma returned from her walk and said to Grandpa, "Grandpa, there's a big beautiful doe standing out in the front yard." Grandpa looked out the front window and sure enough there was the same deer that had been out in the back yard. After lunch Grandpa and Grandma decided to go for a bike ride. They got out their bikes, put on their helmets, and started down the bike trail. Right there by the trail, not far from the house, was the same big deer that had been hanging around the house all morning. She was lying in the tall grasses resting. Grandpa said to Grandma, "This is a very strange acting deer. Deer are wanderers and they don't stay in the same place very long. I wonder if she's sick or something." When they returned from their bike ride Grandpa and Grandma saw that the deer had moved across the road from the house and was nibbling at grass and bushes. All afternoon they saw her four or five more times in different places but still near the house. Grandpa thought to himself, "This is a very, very strange deer." That evening, after dinner and when all the dishes were done, Grandpa and Grandma went out to watch the sunset. When the sun was almost gone and it was getting darker and darker, they saw the really strange deer again. She was walking up the road. When she got near the house she turned and walked into the bushes and tall grass. She was out of sight for a few minutes and then she walked back out of the bushes and onto the road. But this time there was something very different about the strange acting deer. There, right behind her and following very close was a very cute wobbly spotted baby fawn. Grandpa said to Grandma, "So that's why she's been hanging around all day. She had her baby hidden in the bushes all day so that it would be protected from wild animals." But then something else very special happened. Out of the bushes came another very cute wobbly spotted baby fawn. The babies looked like they were only one or two days old. The mother deer took her two babies across the road and fed them, for they were very hungry after hiding all day in the bushes. Then she led the babies down the road and out of sight. She was moving them to a different place so that they would be safe the next day. What a sight Grandpa and Grandma saw that summer. A sight they would never forget.

The End

The Little Runt

A True Story. By Grandpa.

Do you know what a runt is? A runt is usually an animal or thing that is smaller than the others of its kind. Sometimes in a litter of baby kittens, one of the babies is smaller than his or her brothers and sisters. The same is true for puppies, baby mice, baby rats, and even baby pigs. One time Grandpa knew of a family that lived on a farm. One of the things the family raised on the farm was pigs. They had all kinds of pigs. Big pigs, little pigs, white pigs, pink pigs, black pigs, and even spotted pigs. One day, one of the mama pigs had a litter of baby pigs. The little boy in the family liked to watch the little baby pigs because, unlike big pigs, that were usually ugly, dirty and smelly, little pigs were clean and very, very cute. He would sit down by the pigpen and watch the little pigs chasing each other around, sucking milk, and then laying down to sleep all piled up together. The boy noticed a baby pig sleeping all by its self over in the corner of the pen. It was the runt. The little runt was weak from hunger because his bigger brothers and sisters would always push him out of the way and he could never get enough milk to make him strong and healthy. The little runt just lay there shivering from the cold. The boy knew that if the little runt didn't get some help soon, he would surely die. So the boy picked up the little runt and took him up to the house. In the house, he put an old blanket in the bottom of a large cardboard box and shined a heat lamp in it to keep the little runt warm. He fed the little runt some nice warm cow's milk from a baby bottle and put the little runt in the box. Every day, for weeks, the boy would feed the little runt and play with him out in the yard. Soon the little runt grew strong and healthy. He was also getting bigger. He got too big for the box in the house, so the boy put the old blanket outside by the back door and that's where the little runt slept. The little runt no longer needed to drink milk from the baby bottle. He had his own little food bowl right beside his blanket. After a few weeks of living by the back door, the boy thought it was time for the little runt to go back down to the pigpen and live with the other pigs. The boy put the little runt in the pigpen, but the little runt would not have anything to do with the other pigs and just stood by the gate looking at the boy and making sad little grunting noises. He was not happy there and wanted to be with the boy. The boy let the little runt out of the pen and took him back to his blanket by the back door. After that the little runt followed the boy around where ever he went, just like a dog. And when the boy went to school, the little runt would sit out by the mailbox, waiting for the school bus and the boy. Grandpa doesn't know what ever happened to the little runt. But he does know that the little runt was a very lucky little pig. You see, he never got sold to be made into bacon or ham or sausage, like the other pigs. He had become the family pet. Sometimes it's okay to be the smallest or the youngest, isn't it?

The End

The Gold Tooth

A True Story. By Grandpa.

When Grandpa was a little boy, about five or six or so, his baby teeth started to get loose. He was told that they would soon come out and newer and bigger teeth would grow in their place. Well, one day, one tooth got so loose that it easily pulled out. It felt weird to Grandpa to be able to stick his tongue in the hole that used to be a tooth. The tooth that came out was a top front tooth, and when Grandpa looked in the mirror and smiled he thought he looked kind of funny. Anyway, one day a neighbor, Mr. Miller, paid a visit. Now, Mr. Miller had a gold tooth. It was a front tooth, the same tooth that Grandpa had just lost. Every time Mr. Miller smiled, that gold tooth would sparkle and shine, just like a bright star in a black sky. Grandpa thought that gold tooth looked really cool so he asked Mr. Miller, "How did you get that gold tooth?" "Well son," Mr. Miller said, "When I was about your age I started losing teeth just like you are now. I was told that when a tooth came out I was never, ever to stick my tongue in the hole that it came out of and a gold tooth would grow in its place. So I never, ever stuck my tongue in the hole and this gold tooth grew in." Then Mr. Miller smiled at Grandpa, with that big gold tooth sparkling and shining, and asked, "Did you stick your tongue in that hole yet?" Grandpa hung his head and said, "Yes." Then Mr. Miller said, "Well, that's okay. It's too late for that tooth to grow in gold, but when the others come out, don't stick your tongue in the holes and the teeth will grow in gold." Grandpa was really anxious to grow a gold tooth, so when the next tooth came out he really tried to keep his tongue out of the hole. It didn't work. He accidentally stuck his tongue in the hole and ruined any chance for a gold tooth in that one. Grandpa thought to himself, "I'll try harder next time." Once again another tooth came out and Grandpa worked and worked to keep his tongue out of the hole. And once again, it didn't work. Every time Grandpa lost a tooth, he just couldn't seem to keep his tongue out of the holes, and ruined any chance of having a gold tooth. All of his new teeth grew in shiny white. He thought that Mr. Miller must be some kind of a hero to be able to grow a gold tooth. Well, Grandpa finally did get a gold tooth. Three of them, as a matter of fact. You see, when Grandpa was growing up he didn't always brush his teeth after every meal and after eating candy. He didn't always brush his teeth before going to bed like he was supposed to. He didn't always floss either. So when Grandpa grew older, some of his teeth went bad, just like he had been told they would if he didn't take care of them. He had to go to the dentist one day to have the bad teeth removed and replaced with gold ones. It was very expensive and was not very much fun either. Now, Grandpa wishes he had taken better care of his teeth when he was young. This is a true story, but do you think, if you don't stick your tongue in the hole where a tooth is growing back in, will you really grow in a gold tooth? Do you know anyone who has tried it?

The End

Rats

A True Story. By Grandpa.

One day in the spring, Grandma was sitting out on the deck knitting when out of the corner of her eye she saw something move. She looked around and there was a big ol' wood rat scooting across the deck and into the bushes. It had a piece of cat food in its mouth that it had stolen from George the cat's food dish. Grandma got up and went to find Grandpa. "Grandpa," Grandma said, "We have wood rats around the house again and they are stealing George's food." Grandpa said, "Okay," and went out to the shed to get the HAVE-A-HEART trap to catch the thieving rats. Now, a HAVE-A-HEART trap is a little wire cage with a trap door at one end. It doesn't kill the rat like a regular rat trap does, but rather catches them alive so they can be released somewhere far away from the house. Grandpa set up the trap that night and baited it with cat food. The next morning Grandpa and Grandma went to check the trap and sure enough the door had slammed shut and inside was a little brown wood rat, all wide eyed and scared. Grandpa said to the little rat, "don't be worried little fella, I'm not going to hurt you. I'm going to set you free in the woods so that you can start a new home somewhere else, far from my house." So Grandpa and Grandma loaded the trap with the little rat in it into the back of the pickup and drove way out in the woods on an old gravel road. When they came to a little meadow with bushes and tall grass they stopped. Grandpa said to Grandma, "There are plenty of bushes and tall grass for him to hide in and lots of food, so this should be a good place to let him go." Grandpa got the trap out and put it on the ground by some bushes and opened the trap door. The little rat quickly jumped out of the trap and ran towards the bushes, but just before he got there, he turned around and ran back towards Grandpa and the trap. Then he ran out to the middle of the road and then started running down the road as fast as he could go. Just then a big old hawk came swooping down from out of nowhere, flew right over Grandpa's head, and pounced on the hapless little rat just a few feet from where Grandpa was standing. Then the big hawk flew up to the top of a big fir tree with the now dead rat and began to eat his dinner of the day. After watching all this happen, Grandpa and Grandma were amazed at the sight they just saw. But they were also sad that the little rat they worked so hard to keep alive was snatched up by a hungry hawk. They figured that they would have to let the next rat they catch go free in a different spot than this. Because if the big hawk saw them coming again, with the HAVE-A-HEART trap, he would just sit up in a tree and wait for his dinner to be set free.

The End

The Firecracker

A True Story. By Grandpa.

The Fourth of July is the day on which we celebrate the birth of our nation. We celebrate with parades, picnics, barbecues, and in some places, fireworks shows. Some people have small fireworks shows right in their own back yards, with safe fireworks. Grandpa knows of a young boy who got a hold of some unsafe fireworks like big firecrackers and cherry bombs and things like that. These kinds of fireworks make really loud booms and can do a lot of damage if not used properly. Well, the young boy was shooting off his firecrackers when one of them that he was holding in his hand, accidentally exploded early. He was rushed to the emergency room at the hospital where the doctors worked on him. His hand was so badly damaged that he lost all the fingers and thumb of that hand. Now, look at the fingers and thumb on one of your hands and imagine that they were missing. That hand would be useless. You wouldn't be able write with a pencil or color with a crayon or even eat food with a fork. That would not be fun.

Grandpa knows of another young boy who wanted some big, really loud firecrackers. When his father wouldn't let him buy any of the dangerous firecrackers, the young boy said to himself, "I'll make my own big firecrackers." All day long, on the fourth of July, the young boy worked and worked at making a big firecracker. Finally, in the late afternoon the young boy announced to everyone that the firecracker was done, and ready to be blown up. The father didn't think that it was going to work so he said, "Okay, let's see this thing go bang." The boy lit the firecracker. The fuse burned down and all of a sudden the firecracker blew up. But it didn't blow up with a big bang or boom. It blew up with a PPFFTT and sent burning stuff in all different directions. Everybody was busy stomping out the little fires that the burning stuff had started in the dry grass and weeds. After all the little fires were put out, the father decided to check in the garage for any sparks. He opened the door and sure enough, there leaning up against the wall was a broom that was totally on fire. The father grabbed the burning broom and threw it out on the lawn and put out the fire with the garden hose. If he hadn't checked for sparks, the garage surely would have burned down. The young boy learned a valuable lesson that day. Do you know what that lesson was? That's right. Never play with dangerous fireworks, and only do safe fireworks with your parents or other adults. Now, wiggle your fingers and appreciate that you still have them. Oh, and do you happen to know how many stars were on the first American flag?

The End

Pat

A True Story. By Grandpa.

When Grandma was a young girl, about ten years old or so, she lived in the foothills of the San Gabriel Mountains. There weren't very many houses around, just lots of wide-open spaces and lots and lots of wild animals. There were coyotes, rabbits, raccoons, red foxes, hundreds of birds, and yes, even a rattlesnake or two. One day when Grandma was looking out the front window she saw a little baby deer standing on the lawn. Well Grandma was surprised and happy to see the little fawn and she wanted to get a closer look so she quietly eased her way out the front door and stood very still. The little fawn just stood still and looked at her. Grandma kept moving a little closer and a little closer until she was only about ten feet from the cute little guy. The fawn didn't seem to be afraid of Grandma and the two of them just stood there looking at each other. Finally Grandma eased back into the house and the fawn wandered off into the brush. A couple days later the fawn showed up again, and Grandma got even closer to it than she did the first time. The little fawn kept coming back every day or two and each time Grandma would get close to it until one day something was different. Grandma had a small sweet carrot in her hand, which she offered to the little deer. He sniffed at the carrot and finally took it out of her hand and ate it. Grandma kept feeding the fawn, all summer long, whenever he came around. By the end of summer Grandma and the little deer were very good friends and Grandma gave him a name: Pat. Then Pat didn't show up for a

while and Grandma wondered what happened to him. The next spring Grandma looked out the window and saw a deer standing in the front yard eating the tender young flower shoots coming up in the gardens. It was not quite fully-grown and had two little horns sticking out on top of his head. Grandma wondered, "Could that be Pat?" Grandma got a carrot and eased out the front door and slowly walked out into the yard and stood still. The deer looked at Grandma for a minute and then slowly walked over to her. Grandma held out the carrot for the deer and he sniffed at it and then ate it. Grandma said, "Hi Pat, nice to see you. Pat stayed around all summer long and ate almost anything that Grandma offered him. He grew fat and sleek and healthy. There were lots of deer in the mountains, but Grandma could always spot Pat. The second spring Pat showed up with his two horns but this time the horns had two branches indicating that he was two years old. The third year he had three branches. The fourth year he had four branches. The fifth year came and Pat showed up with five branches on each horn. He had grown into a big beautiful buck and Grandma was thrilled when he came over to her for his carrot. That summer Pat stayed around eating carrots and apples and anything else that he took a fancy to. When fall came, Grandma didn't see Pat anymore and she looked forward to spring to see him with six branches on his horns. A neighbor came to Grandma's house and told her family that he had seen some hunters loading a big buck they had just shot, into the back of their pickup truck. Grandma got a sick feeling in her stomach fearing it might be Pat. The next spring came around and Pat did not show up like he always had and Grandma knew then that Pat had ended up on someone's dinner table. She felt really bad because she had made a friend out of a wild animal. He had lost all fear of humans and was easy prey when hunting season came. After that Grandma just watched and enjoyed the beautiful wild animals and did not try to make friends or tame them. That is something for all of us to remember.

The End

The Little Bird

A True Story. By Grandpa.

Out in front of Grandpa and Grandma's house are three bird feeders. The first bird feeder holds millet seeds for wrens, house finches, juncos, chickadees, and so on. The second one holds small black sunflower seeds that attract black birds, nuthatches, and doves. The third one holds thistle seeds that goldfinches and pine siskins love. The other day Grandpa was watching the birds through the front window and he noticed that the thistle feeder was a little low. Grandpa got the thistle seed bag and went out to where the feeders are. He set the seed sack down on the ground so that he could get the bird feeder down to fill it. As Grandpa stood back up to get the bird feeder, there, right in front of him, and less than an arm's length away was a little pine siskin sitting on the bottom part of the feeder. Grandpa stopped and stood real still, looking at the little guy, who was cocking his head from side to side, looking back at Grandpa. Grandpa couldn't believe this wild little creature didn't fly away. After a little bit, Grandpa said to him, "Hi little siskin, mind if I fill your feeder?" The siskin just sat there, cocking his head from side to side, looking at Grandpa. Finally Grandpa decided to try something he had never tried before. He slowly raised his hand up under the bird feeder with his finger sticking out. Grandpa's hand was about six inches from the siskin and the little guy still didn't move. He just sat there looking at Grandpa, right in the eye. Grandpa kept inching his finger up toward the little bird until finally he touched its little chest.

Just like a tame bird or parakeet he jumped on Grandpa's finger. Grandpa couldn't believe this was happening. He held the siskin at arm's length, looking at him, and the siskin looked back at Grandpa. Grandpa held him like that for so long that his arm was starting to get tired. All during the time the bird was on Grandpa's finger, Grandpa softly talked to him. He wanted to yell for Grandma to come and see, but he didn't dare because that might scare the little bird. Finally the little bird decided to fly off and left Grandpa standing there dumbfounded from what had just happened. A lot of strange things have happened in Grandpa's life, and this one ranks right up there near the top. Now, see how close you can get to a bird before it flies away. Be gentle and good luck.

The End

Old Scratchy

A True Story. By Grandpa.

On the farm that Grandpa grew up on, there were a whole bunch of different kinds of animals. You know the kinds of animals that live on farms. Milk cows, beef cattle, pigs, chickens for laying eggs, and chickens for making fried chicken. There were rabbits, goats, ducks, watch dogs, and cats. All the animals were tame and could be petted and held. All the animals, that is, except for, the cats. The cats were not house cats. They were barn cats, and they lived in the barn where they could catch mice and birds. They also loved the fresh, warm cow's milk that Grandpa would give them every morning and every night when he milked the cows. You couldn't get close to them or pet them because they were just about the wildest and meanest cats Grandpa ever knew. The meanest cat of the bunch, Grandpa named Scratchy.

Grandpa gave him that name because when the kitten was real small, Grandpa picked him up to pet him, and the little kitten scratched his hand really bad. Grandpa never touched the cat after that. It was the same day after day. Grandpa would go out to milk the cows, morning and night, and there would be old Scratchy and the other wild cats waiting for their fresh warm cow's milk.

Then one day when Grandpa went out to milk the cows, old Scratchy didn't show up for his daily, warm cow's milk. Days, weeks, and months went by and old Scratchy never did come for his milk. Grandpa figured that something bad had happened to the

cat. Maybe he just went off and died, or maybe a coyote got him, or maybe he just went to live at another nearby farm. Who knows where old Scratchy went off to. Even though Scratchy was a mean and wild cat Grandpa kind of missed him at milking time. Then one day Grandpa was milking the cows when he heard a cat meow really loud. He turned around and, by-golly, there was old Scratchy standing by the milk dish begging for fresh, warm cow's milk. Grandpa got up to pour him some milk and old Scratchy came over purring and started rubbing his head against Grandpa's leg. Grandpa leaned over and patted Scratchy on the head and Scratchy just kept on purring. Grandpa poured him some milk and Scratchy let Grandpa pet his back while he was lapping up his milk. Grandpa couldn't believe it. What had changed mean old Scratchy to be a nice tame pussy-cat? Grandpa never could figure this puzzle out. Maybe this wasn't old Scratchy at all. Maybe it was just a stray kitty that looked like him. What do you think?

The End

The Boy & the River
A True Story. By Grandpa.

One summer when school was out, a man took his two sons and a couple of their friends to a cabin on a river in the mountains. They planned on rafting the river in front of the cabin and hiking in the woods, which they did. The second day the boys asked the man to take them further up the river so that they could have a longer ride. The man took the boys and the raft about two miles up the river. He put the raft in the water and said that he would ride the raft down first. He got in the raft and asked one of the friends if he wanted to go. The boy said yes and threw his life jacket in the raft and got in. The man pushed off and away they went. They drifted for a while until they came to a bend in the river. As they rounded the bend they saw a horrible sight. Right in front of them all they could see was white water, waves, rapids and water falls. Just then they hit a big rock and raft tipped over and the two of them were thrown into the raging water. Neither one had their life jackets on. The boy had a hold of the raft and as he surfaced he saw the top of a windfallen tree sticking out over the river. He grabbed the tree and was swung into the bank by the swift water and he crawled out to safety. The boy didn't know what happened to the man. He knew he was in trouble because now he was on the opposite side of the river, away from the road and help. He couldn't cross over to the other side because of the deep rushing water. He couldn't follow the river down to the cabin because big cliffs were in the way. He couldn't hike out in another direction because he didn't know which way to

go and would surely get lost. He decided to stay put and wait to be rescued if possible. He turned the raft upside down and made a bed of fir and cedar boughs under it just in case he had to stay overnight. The other boys had been waiting down river for the man and the boy to arrive in the raft, but they never showed up. So the other boys eventually called the sheriff, who in turn called the Coast Guard to help search the river for the missing man and boy. The Coast Guard helicopter spotted the boy on the bank of the river and led the sheriff and other rescuers to where he was. The rescuers yelled across the raging water to the boy and told him to hike upstream a short distance to where there was a small footbridge that crossed the river. The bridge had a gate that was padlocked shut so someone got a bolt cutter, opened the gate and the boy was saved. The man was later found downstream. He had drowned. This story has a happy and sad ending. Happy because the boy was found alive and well. Sad because the man had lost his life. But most importantly we have all learned some valuable lessons in this story. Lesson one: we should never swim or float a river that we haven't checked out first. Lesson two:

always wear a lifejacket when on or near the water. And lesson three: if you ever get lost or separated from your family or friends, do like the boy did and stay put, and wait to be rescued. I sure am glad that the wind fallen tree was sticking out over the river that day.

The End

The Last Grizzly Bear

A True Story. By Grandpa.
(As Told To Grandpa By Great Grandma)

Back in the olden days, before there were cars and television and smartphones and things like that, there lived a man, Uncle Gene, and his wife Anna. They lived on a ranch in the hills overlooking a valley with a little town in it. The town was then known as "The Indiana Settlement," but is known today as Pasadena, California. Out in front of their house was a dirt road that people traveled on with their horses and wagons. Sometimes the people would stop at Uncle Gene's house to water their horses and rest for a while. So when Aunt Anna saw dust from the horses and wagons down in the valley she would whip up a batch of biscuits and asked Uncle Gene to go get some honey out of the bee hives behind the house. By the time the people got to the house there would be hot biscuits and fresh honey waiting for them to snack on. What a treat. One day Aunt Anna asked Uncle Gene to get some fresh honey for the biscuits. When he got to the bee hives they were all knocked over and half the honey had been eaten. Uncle Gene thought to himself, what mysterious thing could have done this to my beehives. A few days later Uncle Gene found out what the mysterious thing was.

When he went to get some honey he found a big grizzly bear knocking over his beehives again and eating his honey. The mean and dangerous bear turned and growled and showed his big, ugly, stained teeth. Then the big bear turned and started toward Uncle Gene with his big mouth agape and drool hanging down in long threads. He growled really loud and stomped his front feet on the ground as a warning. Uncle Gene was afraid for his life. He ran to the house and got a rifle. He told everyone to stay in the house because there was a mean and dangerous bear outside and he was mad. Uncle Gene went back outside and there was the bear eating honey again. When the bear saw Gene he turned and started running towards him. Uncle Gene raised the rifle and, BOOM, shot the bear. The bear didn't die but instead ran up a canyon and over some hills and disappeared. Uncle Gene got five or six other men to help him track the bear down. They searched up canyons, over mountains and everywhere, no bear. They looked here and looked there and still no bear. Where could he be? Finally on the third day of searching they found the wounded bear. He was under a scrub oak tree lying down because he was weak from losing so much blood. The men killed him and took him back to town. The bear measured eight feet. That's as tall as Grandpa's living room. Well, it turns out that the bear was the last grizzly bear in Southern California, and Uncle Gene had shot him. Grizzly bears still exist in places like Canada, Northern Idaho, and Montana, in Yellowstone Park, but not in California. It's been said that Uncle Gene charged twenty-five cents apiece for people to have their picture taken with the bear. I wonder how much money he made that day.

The End

What If

A True Story. By Grandpa.

Did you ever think: what if I was something other than who I am? Grandpa has. One time Grandpa was watching the little swallows flying up in the sky over his house and he thought to himself, "What if I was a bird? It sure would be fun to and fly around up there, swooping and soaring and darting around." Then Grandpa thought, "But if I was a bird, I would have to eat bugs and worms and things like that. YUK! That would not be fun." Grandpa decided he would not like to be a bird. Now, can you think of some other things that might be fun to be other than what you are? Just think. What if you were a beagle dog? You could chase balls and frisbees and cats. You could lie around all day taking naps, not doing anything and eating dog food any time you wanted.

"EATING DOG FOOD? YUK!" said Grandpa to himself, "That would not be fun." Grandpa decided he didn't want to be a beagle dog either. Just think. What if you were a kitty? Kitties get to lie around all day too. They sleep and yawn and stretch. They climb trees, chase birds and mice, and just have a good time. But kitties also get chased. They get chased by dogs and that would not be fun. So Grandpa thought he would definitely not want to be a kitty.

Just think. What if you were an otter? Otters have fun all the time. They play games every day with each other. They slide down hills in the snow and swim in rivers and lakes and streams. They even swim in the wintertime in cold icy water. "COLD ICY WATER?" thought Grandpa, "That would not be fun. I don't think I would like to be an otter." What if you were a cheetah? Cheetah's are very fast and can run up to 70 miles per hour or about as fast as your mom and dad drive down the highway in the car. Wouldn't that be fun to be able to run as fast as a car? But cheetah's live in the hot, hot, and dry deserts of Africa where there is no air-conditioning to keep cool by. "NO AIR-CONDITIONING?" said Grandpa. "I don't think I would like to be a cheetah." What if you were an eagle? Eagles soar way up in the blue sky hardly ever flapping their wings twisting and turning back and forth looking for food. Eagles have very sharp eye-sight and can see the slightest movement from a long way away. But eagles get chased by crows that try to pull out their tail feathers. That would not be fun. So Grandpa thought, "I don't think I would like to be an eagle either." Then Grandpa thought, "Maybe I don't want to be something else. Maybe I just like being who I am."

Now, think of something else that you might like to be and then, think of why it might, or might not, be fun being that thing.

The End

Ice Cream

A True Story. By Grandpa.

One year, long, long ago, a family living in southern California decided to spend their Christmas vacation in old Mexico. They rented a "casa," or little house, in a little village way down in Mexico. All the people that lived in the little village were very poor. The village had no electricity, so there were no TV sets or radios, or even computers. There was no running water in the town, so all water had to be dipped out of a well dug into the ground. All these town people were happy, though, because they didn't know anything different. They had never seen electrical things like electric drills, electric saws, refrigerators, and electric lights. Just think. No electric lights on Christmas trees in that village. Now, the little family decided to take their hand cranked ice-cream mixer with them to make ice cream for Christmas. Next door to the house they had rented in the poor little village was a shack, and living in that shack was a family with four little kids. They thought it would be nice to invite the four little kids over for ice cream when it was made, as the little kids had never tasted ice cream before. The little village that they were staying in was located way out in the desert of Mexico, so the father had to drive about fifty miles away to buy a block of ice to make the ice-cream. The roads in Mexico were not very good, so the trip was long dusty and hot, but he got the block of ice and made it back to the little village with the block of ice. The next morning the family started making the ice cream. They put all of the ingredients into the mixer can, plus they ground up candy canes so that the ice cream would be peppermint-flavored. Yum. Then they chipped ice off of the block of ice and packed it around the can in the mixer, dropped salt onto the ice, and started cranking. They cranked and cranked. They took turns cranking because their arms got tired, but pretty soon they had two quarts of homemade ice cream. The mother sent her little girl to invite the four little kids next door, over for ice cream. When she opened the front door to go, there, in the front yard, stood all the little children of the village, about one hundred of them in all. Word had gotten out that the Americans were making ice cream that day, and they were all hoping to get a taste. They each had a cup in their hands. There were chipped glass cups, dented tin cups, cracked plastic cups, and all kinds of things that might hold ice cream. Well, the family looked at each other and decided that they couldn't disappoint all these little kids. They started dishing out ice cream, a little bit at a time to each kid, but there were so many kids that they soon ran out. They put

more ice cream ingredients and ground up candy canes into the mixer can, added more ice and salt, and started cranking again. Soon they had another two quarts of ice cream that they dished out to some of the other little kids. But there were still too many kids and not enough ice cream. They made another batch, and another, and another, until they ran out of the ice cream ingredients and candy canes. There were still more kids waiting and the family thought, what are we going to do? Then the mother got a can of peaches, which they chopped up, and a box of powdered milk, and started making peach ice cream out of that. When the peaches ran out, they chopped up canned pineapple and made pineapple ice cream. Soon all the little kids of the village had been treated to the wonderful American homemade ice cream, and were very happy. But you know what? The American family had run out of canned fruit and powdered milk, so now there was nothing left to make ice cream with. Even the block of ice was gone. Well, the family didn't get their ice cream that Christmas vacation. But they got something even better. They got to treat all those little kids to their first taste of ice cream.

The End

www.ingramcontent.com/pod-product-compliance
Lightning Source LLC
Chambersburg PA
CBHW060458240426
43661CB00006B/844